Yorkshire Cricket

£1

Yorkshire Cricket

A Pictorial Survey

by

Tony Woodhouse and Ron Yeomans

with a foreword by Sir Kenneth Parkinson

DALESMAN BOOKS
1974

The Dalesman Publishing Company Ltd.,

Clapham (via Lancaster), North Yorkshire

First published 1974

© Text, Tony Woodhouse & Ron Yeomans 1974.

ISBN: 0 85206 237 0

Printed by Galava Printing Company Limited, Hallam Road Nelson Lancs.

Contents

The front cover pictures show
(left) Roger Iddison, Yorkshire's first appointed captain in 1863,
and (right) Geoffrey Boycott, the present captain.

Foreword

by Sir Kenneth Parkinson

President of the Yorkshire County Cricket Club

THIS work by Ron Yeomans and Tony Woodhouse is a delightful pictorial history of Yorkshire cricket from 1863 to date. The authors have chosen the pictures and written the script, dividing the years into four periods: Before 1900; Up to World War 1; Between the Wars; and Post-War. The first two are by Tony Woodhouse and the second two by Ron Yeomans, and they have taken particular care not to stress one period more than another.

To the best of my knowledge this book is unique, and is the first pictorial history of Yorkshire cricket ever produced. It contains scores of pictures, including many rare ones, and is a handsome publication which will appeal to all lovers of cricket quite apart from Yorkshiremen.

The Early Days

THE first generally recognised match played by Yorkshire was against Norfolk in 1833. Before this a county eleven of sorts had represented the county and cricket was known to have been played in many towns and villages during the 18th century. However, very little is known of the standard of play and details of the players taking part are very sparse. The first great names in Yorkshire cricket were Tom Marsden and Henry Sampson of Sheffield and that first great pair of bowlers, Ikey Hodgson and William Slinn.

The All-England Eleven and other similar touring teams spread the gospel of cricket around Britain from the later 1840s and did much to popularise the game. As the railways were also extending, county clubs began to be formed throughout the land. Yorkshire were not far behind and the County Cricket Club we know to-day was launched at the Adelphi Hotel in Sheffield in 1863. It was the city of steel that dominated the club—not always to the rest of the county's gratification—for the next thirty years. It would be idle to pretend that these early days were particularly auspicious, although Roger Iddison, Yorkshire's first captain, led his team to become "Champion County". This was mainly due to the club's great fast bowler, George Freeman, and his partner—left-arm fast bowler, Tom Emmett. The latter has been canonised in cricket circles as the original in many after-dinner cricket stories.

Yorkshire spent the next twenty years in comparative obscurity to the chagrin of their many supporters. These early cricketers were certainly characters and there always seemed to be the nucleus of a great team. This could only be expected with such names as Ephraim Lockwood, doyen of the cut; Alan Hill, a potentially great fast bowler; Edmund Peate, the first of a long line of great left-arm slow bowlers; and George Pinder of Ecclesfield, almost unrivalled behind the stumps. There were also the Greenwoods and Eastwood and later that great contrasting opening pair, George Ulyett and Louis Hall.

Unfortunately, these players all too rarely produced the consistency that was expected of them. A succession of professional captains did little to foster team spirit and the fielding was often lax. It took several years of the Hon. Martin Bladen —later Lord Hawke—to knock the team into shape and produce a radical improvement both on and off the field. When at last Lord Hawke led Yorkshire to their first championship title in 1893, it coincided with a fairer distribution of seats on the Committee; the opening of the Headingley ground; and also improved wages, winter pay and improved benefits. It was Lord Hawke, more than anyone else, who harnessed Yorkshire cricket into what is now a tradition of true greatness.

Darnall Cricket Ground, Sheffield, from a painting by Robert Cruickshank, in 1827. This was one of several big grounds in Sheffield, let alone Yorkshire, on which important matches of the time were played.

One of Yorkshire's earliest well-known batsmen, George Anderson of Bedale, achieved more fame as a player with the All-England XI, than he did with the county. Something of a rebel, in 1865 he declined to play for Yorkshire during the disagreement between North and South professional cricketers. It was said of him that he was so enthusiastic about cricket that he took his bat to bed with him.

Roger Iddison, Yorkshire's first appointed captain, in 1863 after the County Club's formation. He led Yorkshire for eight seasons, including 1867 and 1870, when they were undefeated "champions". During this period, Iddison, strangely enough, also played county cricket for Lancashire.

In his prime.

George Freeman, native of Boroughbridge, was Yorkshire's first fast bowler of whom the great Dr. W. G. Grace once said, "He is the greatest fast bowler I've ever met". He was unable to play regularly in the Yorkshire team because of his profession as an auctioneer.

In later years.

Joseph Rowbotham of Sheffield, early Yorkshire batsman, who scored the second recorded century for Yorkshire in a county match. This was against Nottinghamshire at Sheffield in 1869. Our picture shows Rowbotham in 1860, the year before his first appearance for the county.

Later in life, Rowbotham was the licensee for many years of the New Inn, Ecclesall Road, Sheffield, not far from the Bramall Lane ground. The inn is still there. In the background is St. Mary's Church, a well known landmark which could be seen from the pavilion at "the Lane".

J. Rowbotham.
Yorkshire County Cricketer 1860

Yorkshire's first left arm slow bowler, Edmund Peate, native of Holbeck. He was not much of a batsman, but once in a Test Match against Australia, on being reproached for getting out at a crucial stage of the game, he commented, "Aye, but I could not trust Mr. Studd". At that time, Mr. C. T. Studd was one of the leading amateur batsmen in England. His wickets for Yorkshire cost 12.55 runs each—less than those of any other regular Yorkshire bowler.

The Yorkshire Team of 1877.

An early Yorkshire wicket-keeper, George Pinder of Ecclesfield, Sheffield, was considered one of the finest wicket-keepers of his day.

"Why, he's more fit to eat a penny cake than play cricket." This was alleged to have been said of Ephraim Lockwood (pictured here) by spectators at the Oval in 1868, on Lockwood's first appearance for Yorkshire, when he opened the batting with his uncle, John Thewlis. Both batsmen were products of the famous Lascelles Hall Cricket Club, well known as the nursery of Yorkshire cricket. In the match at the Oval, Lockwood and Thewlis joined together in a partnership worth 176 runs.

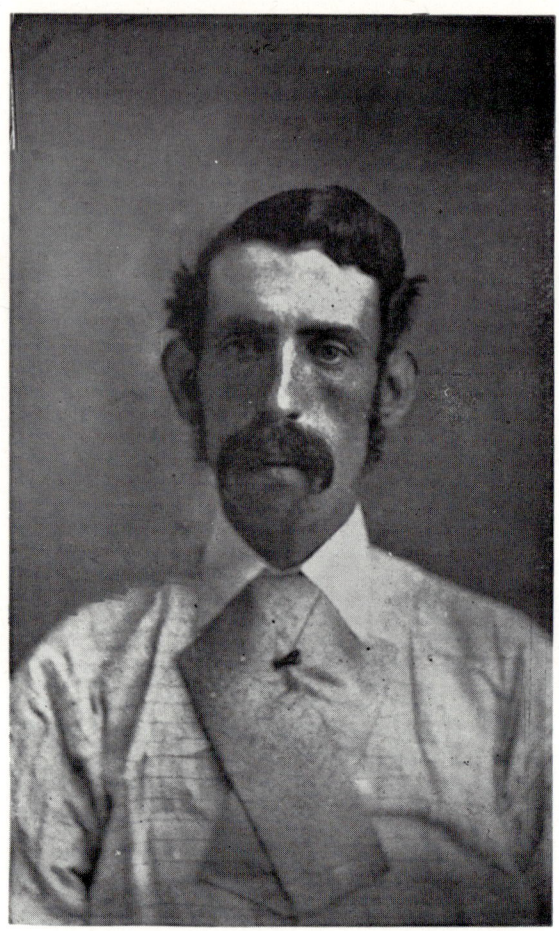

"Happy Jack," George Ulyett, aggressive opening batsman, with a record for big hitting. One of the few Sheffield products for Yorkshire cricket during the last 100 years. Also a fast bowler, good enough to open the attack for England against Australia.

Louis Hall, Sunday School teacher from Batley, famed as a Yorkshire opening batsman. He had the reputation of being a "blocker" and the records show that he carried his bat through a completed innings on more occasions than any other Yorkshire batsman.

This is Lockwood Viaduct at Huddersfield, close to the present Lockwood cricket ground. In the latter half of the last century, the mighty Australian hitter, G. J. Bonnor, threw a cricket ball over this viaduct for a bet.

Bobby Peel, all-rounder from Churwell and Rhodes's immediate predecessor as a left arm slow bowler. Scored 210 not out in Yorkshire's record score of 887 against Warwickshire in 1896.

19

The Golden Age

LORD Hawke, Yorkshire's first great captain, had an eleven during his period of leadership which could compare favourably with any other county's during any period of cricket history. This is not at all surprising when one considers that Hirst and Rhodes, arguably the two greatest all-rounders ever to have appeared, were leading members of his side. Hirst remains the only player ever to have scored over 2,000 runs and taken 200 wickets in a season, and Rhodes has more wickets to his credit than any other bowler.

George Herbert Hirst, ever-reliable in a crisis, was literally worshipped by cricket lovers everywhere—not only Yorkshiremen. No schoolboy could possibly model himself on a better player and man than this worthy character. Wilfred Rhodes on the other hand was almost taciturn in manner and never suffered fools gladly, but had a cricket brain feared and respected by all. Any cricket eleven with two such players in its ranks would have only needed a few average players to reach the front rank.

Yet this Yorkshire side also had a great opening pair in J. T. Brownsen and John Tunnicliffe. The latter was unrivalled as a slip-fielder in those days. Schofield Haigh was a medium-paced off-spinner, devastating on a wicket that suited him and a batsman good enough to reach his 1,000 runs in a season. Bobby Peel, Rhodes' predecessor, and Ted Wainwright were both England all-rounders and

David Hunter was considered most unfortunate never to have kept wicket in Test Cricket. In David Denton, Yorkshire possessed an attacking batsman in the same mould as J. T. Tyldesley, and he was also a wonderful outfielder. Before the war two young all-rounders appeared on the scene in Major Booth and Alonzo Drake who but for hostilities and illness would undoubtedly have made great names for themselves.

Without its "Gentlemen"—and amateurs were of the aristocracy or pretty close to it in those Edwardian days—the Golden Age would not have possessed so many batsmen of style and elegance. Yorkshire had a surprisingly large number of top class amateurs but apart from his lordship, none was able to play very regularly. The Hon. F. S. Jackson did lead England with great success, but his cricket for Yorkshire was curtailed by his political career. T. L. Taylor and Frank Mitchell were both extremely fine batsmen and Ernest Smith and Clem and Rockley Wilson were all-rounders of the highest calibre.

This plethora of talent, ably led by Lord Hawke, especially during the period 1900-1902, could certainly be termed the strongest county side ever mustered. When one remembers that this was cricket's Golden Age—yes, the age of Ranji, Fry and Richardson—then is there really any doubt that this Yorkshire team have never been surpassed?

Lord Hawke, Yorkshire's greatest-ever cricketing personality. He captained the side from 1883 to 1910 and was President from 1898 to 1938. This picture is taken from the original painted by Shirley Slocombe in 1903.

RECORD SCORE IN FIRST CLASS CRICKET.

YORKSHIRE v. WARWICKSHIRE,

Played at Birmingham on May 7th, 8th & 9th, 1896

YORKSHIRE.   RUNS AS SCORED

Mr. F. S. Jackson — 4 1 2 1 1 1 4 2 1 4 4 4 4 1 1 4 3 4 2 3 1
2 2 1 2 1 4 1 4 1 1 4 1 1 2 1 1 1 4 2 2 1 1 1 1 1 1 1 1 1
1 2 4 2 1 3 3 1 c Law b Ward   117

Tunnicliffe — 4 3 2 1 1 4 4 3 2 4 c Pallett b Glover   28

Brown   1 1 2 2 4 3 1 2 1 2 3 1 c Hill b Pallett   23

Denton — 4 1 1 c W G. Quaife b Santall.......................   6

Moorhouse — 1 4 1 1 1 3 1 4 4 4 1 2 1 4 2 1 1 2 2 4 1 1 1 1
1 1 1 1 4 4 2 1 1 4 1 2 b Ward   72

Wainwright   1 1 2 2 2 1 1 4 1 3 1 2 1 1 1 4 4 3 1 4 4 1 4
4 1 2 2 2 2 1 4 3 1 1 1 2 4 4 4 2 2 1 2 1 4 1 1 1 1 4 4 1 4
1 1 4 1 1 1 1 run out   126

Peel — 4 2 3 2 2 1 3 4 4 2 1 4 1 2 1 1 2 2 8 1 1 1 1 1 1 1 1
1 4 1 1 1 1 2 3 1 4 1 1 1 3 1 4 1 8 4 1 4 2 3 2 1 4 1 2 1
1 1 2 1 1 1 2 1 3 1 4 4 2 2 1 1 3 1 1 3 3 3 1 3 4 2 1
2 5 8 1 1 1 4 1 1 1 1 4 2 1 1 1 1 1 1 1 2 1 not out   210

Mr. F. W. Milligan — 4 4 4 4 1 4 1 4 3 4 1 b Pallett   34

Lord Hawke — 3 1 2 1 1 4 1 4 2 1 4 3 4 4 4 2 1 3 1 4 1 8
1 4 1 4 1 4 2 1 1 1 1 3 1 2 3 2 4 1 1 4 1 1 1 1 2 1 1
4 1 1 2 2 2 1 2 1 1 3 1 4 4 1 4 2 1 1 4 4 2 b Pallett   166

Hirst — 4 1 2 2 4 1 1 1 4 1 1 4 1 1 1 1 1 4 4 1 1 1 4 1 1
1 3 4 1 4 1 4 1 4 c Glover b Santall   85

Hunter — 1 2 1 1 b Pallett..   5

     b 2 1 1 1, l b 1 2 1 1, w 1 1 1 1   15
                                     ———

Hits.   1-5   102-4's   34-3's   71-2's   215-singles   15 extras.   887
Duration of Innings 10 hours 50 minutes.

FALL OF WICKETS.

1 wkt for 63, 2-124, 3-141, 4-211 5-339, 6-405, 7-448, 8-740, 9-876, 10-887

WARWICKSHIRE.   1ST INNINGS.   2ND INNINGS

	1ST INNINGS	2ND INNINGS
1 Mr. H W Bainbridge	c Hunter b Hirst...... 5	b Wainwright........ 29
2 Quaife	...... b Hirst 0	not out 18
3 Quaife (W. G.)	...... not out 92	
4 Law	...... c Jackson b Hirst ... 7	
5 Lilley	...... b Hirst 0	
6 Mr J. E. Hill	...... b Hirst 4	
6 Diver ...	...... b Peel 27	
7 Pallett	...... c Wain'right b Jackson 25	
9 Santall	...... b Hirst 29	
10 Mr. A. C. S. Glover	b Hirst...... 1	
11 Ward	...... b Hirst...... 3	
	b 4, l-b 3, w1, n-b 2, 10	b , l-b , w , n-b 1 1

             TOTAL... 203   TOTAL.... 48

1 wkt for 0, 2 , 7- 3- 25, 4- 25, 5- 31, 6- 78, 7-117, 8-170, 9-176, 10-203

1 wkt for 48.

BOWLING ANALYSIS.

YORKSHIRE.—First Innings.

	Overs	M'd'ns	Runs	Wkts		Overs	M'd'ns	Runs	Wkts
Santall	65	9	223	2	J. E. Hill	3	0	14	0
Ward	62	11	175	2	H. W. Bainbridge	6	1	17	0
A. C. S. Glover ...	30	1	154	1	Lilley	8	1	13	0
Pallett	75	3	184	4	Quaife (W.) ...	9	1	18	0
Quaife (W.G.) ...	8	1	33	0	Diver	10	1	41	0

Pallett bowled two wides, and Diver and Hill one each.

WARWICKSHIRE.—First Innings.

	Overs	M'd'ns	Runs	Wkts		Overs	M'd'ns	Runs	Wkts
Hirst	40	16	59	8	F. W. Milligan...	13	5	14	0
Peel	31	21	27	1	Brown	4	0	24	0
F S Jackson ...	18	8	23	1	Moorhouse	4	1	11	0
Wainright ...	16	7	35	0					

Hirst and Moorhouse each bowled a no-ball, and Peel one wide

SECOND INNINGS.

	Overs	M'd'ns	Runs	Wkts		Overs	M'd'ns	Runs	Wkts
F. W. Milligan	5	1	15	0	Peel	5	2	4	0
Moorhouse	4	0	24	0	Wainwright	2-1	1	4	1

Moorhouse bowled a no-ball.

A copy of a special score card of the Yorkshire v Warwickshire match at Edgbaston, Birmingham, in 1896, showing Yorkshire's record score of 887, made in 10 hours 50 minutes, including no less than four centuries. Unfortunately, Yorkshire batted too long to force a win.

Probably the best wicket-keeper who never played in a Test Match, David Hunter is high up in the line of great Yorkshire 'keepers. A native of Scarborough, Hunter's pastime was the breeding of canaries.

T. Mycroft J. B. Wostinholm (Sec.)   Rhodes   Tunnicliffe   Hunter   Whitehead J. Hoyland (Scorer) A. Shaw

Wainwright   T. L. Taylor   Lord Hawke (Captain)   Haigh   Hirst

Brown   Denton

The Yorkshire Team that won the County Championship in 1900, the first
of a hat-trick of championship wins.

Sir Stanley Jackson, son of Yorkshire and England's captain. In 1905, he topped both batting and bowling averages for England v Australia and led the side to a 3–2 victory. He is the only batsman who has scored five centuries against Australia in Test Matches in England.

Yours Sincerely,
G. H. Hirst

George Hirst in his prime.

George Hirst of Kirkheaton ranks with Rhodes as being Yorkshire's greatest ever all-rounder. Ever remembered for his performance in 1906 of scoring over 2,000 runs and obtaining over 200 wickets. Once scored 341 runs against Leicestershire in 1905 and twice performed the hat-trick against the same county. His autograph is shown opposite.

George Hirst in his later years.

Another product of Huddersfield, Schofield Haigh was a great friend of George Hirst and like him was a stalwart of the Yorkshire team during their golden years.

T. L. Taylor, once chosen for England against Australia, but he stood down. He seemed likely to achieve fame for Yorkshire as a batsman, but business took him away from the game.

The figure on left is J. T. Brown of Darfield (do not confuse with the J. T. Brown of Driffield), fast bowler, whose promising career for Yorkshire was cut short by injuries. Had a reputation as a hard-hitting batsman. Later played in league cricket.

A snapshot of the great Wilfred Rhodes taken during the luncheon interval "parade" at Lord's at one of his early Test Matches there.

Wilfred Rhodes and David Denton snapped together at the height of their careers. Rhodes, the great all-rounder, achieved the cricketers' double on 16 occasions. Denton, fine batsman and outfield, scored over 33,000 runs for Yorkshire in his career and on 20 occasions passed the 1,000 runs mark in a season.

Rhodes and Denton chatting over
former days of cricketing glory.

Every year Lord Hawke, as captain of Yorkshire, entertained members of his team, as well as Yorkshire Committee members and wives and friends, to a party at his seat at Wighill Park near Tadcaster. This group shows the party at Wighill in 1909. Unfortunately the house has how been demolished, but Lord Hawke's ground still remains and is used by the Wighill Park team.

Another Yorkshire cricketing group—the team of 1911—but it was a lean year for Yorkshire and they finished seventh in the county championship table. The team comprises:—Top row: Williams, Bates, Booth, Wilson, Drake, Hoyland; Centre: Sir A. White, Denton, E. J. Radcliffe, Haigh, Hirst, Rhodes; Bottom: R. Kilner, Dolphin.

Alonzo Drake took 482 wickets for
Yorkshire before World War 1 and
scored three centuries, but ill-health
brought an early death.

Did you know a Yorkshire cricketer once won the Grand National? He was Major J. P. Wilson (pictured here) who appeared a few times for the county in 1911-12. His winning horse was Double Chance in 1925.

38

Major Booth, another fine all-rounder for the county, who was a casualty in world war 1 when at the height of his career.

He took 558 wickets for Yorkshire and one of his two centuries was 210 runs against Worcestershire in 1911.

He was a native of Pudsey and the picture on this page shows the house where he spent many years of his life and where his sister is reputed to have kept a room for him in the hope of his return, even many years after he was known to have been killed. A stained glass window to his memory is in St. Lawrence's Church, Pudsey.

Between the Wars

THE season of 1919, the first year after World War 1, was one of two-day county cricket with hours of play from 11.30 a.m. to 7.30 p.m. Long before the season was over, the idea was considered unsuccessful because of the hours, not appreciated by the cricketing public, and because of the late travelling involved for the players. But Yorkshire won the county championship, and indeed were to finish in top position on no less than 12 occasions between the wars.

In 1919, the Yorkshire team, which had suffered the loss of their two main bowlers, Booth and Drake, found a match-winner in Waddington, while Rhodes, now 41 years old, took on a new lease of life. On five more occasions before his retirement, he achieved the cricketers' double of 1,000 runs and 100 wickets. Holmes and Sutcliffe became household names in cricket as Yorkshire's opening pair, while Emmot Robinson, a "new boy" at 35 years of age, took the first of his 832 wickets for Yorkshire.

Macaulay became a regular in the Yorkshire attack in 1920, with D. C. F. Burton in the second year of a three-year reign as Yorkshire captain. In 1922, Yorkshire won the championship again, the first of four consecutive victories. By 1923, Leyland, probably the greatest ever left-handed batsman to play for Yorkshire, had become an established county player. Some of the players that were later to make Yorkshire a great side under the leadership of A. B. Sellers were now edging in to the team—Mitchell, Barber and Wood, who replaced Dolphin as wicket-keeper in 1928; Bowes, after an apprenticeship at Lord's in 1929; and Verity in 1930. Verity topped the Yorkshire averages and was a fine bowler in his first season, just as four years later, in 1934, Hutton hit the headlines in his first season with the team.

A Yorkshire tragedy was the death of Roy Kilner in the spring of 1928. He died from an illness contracted while on an overseas cricket tour the previous winter. In 1934, Yorkshire had another established all-rounder in Smailes and what became the Sellers' "circus" was now complete. Officially appointed captain in 1933, he led the team to the top of the county championship on five occasions between the wars—six, if 1932 is included, as Sellers deputised for Greenwood practically throughout that season.

Yorkshire dropped to sixth position in the table in 1934, but Leyland, Sutcliffe, Verity and Bowes were regularly away playing for England. Yet in that season, six batsmen scored over 1,000 runs and three bowlers took over 100 wickets. In 1938, Yorkshire had no less than five players in the England team against Australia at the Oval. The war came, and this great Yorkshire side of the 1930's was fated never to play together again.

A. Dolphin   R. Kilner   A. Waddington   A. C. Williams   H. Sutcliffe

G. H. Hirst   W. R. Rhodes   D. E. F. Burton   E. R. Wilson   D. Denton

P. Holmes   Captain   E. Robinson

The Yorkshire Championship Winning Team of 1919.

Percy Holmes drives in the nets.

Herbert Sutcliffe plays a ball to leg.

A composite picture showing (left) the score board after Brown and Tunnicliffe had shared an opening partnership worth 554 runs against Derbyshire at Chesterfield in 1898, and (right) the record broken in 1932, when Holmes and Sutcliffe scored 555 runs together for Yorkshire's first wicket against Essex at Leyton.

A picture of Herbert Sutcliffe taken
when he was a boy of 14.

In the early days after World War I, E. R. Wilson came in to the Yorkshire side from schoolmastering at Winchester and proved himself such an accurate slow bowler that he was chosen to go with the M.C.C. team to Australia in 1920-21.

YORKSHIRE COUNTY CRICKET CLUB,
Headingley Ground, Leeds.

SOUVENIR OFFICIAL SCORE CARD.

YORKSHIRE v. LANCASHIRE, Saturday, Monday, Tuesday, June 7, 9, 10, 1924.

LANCASHIRE.

First Innings.			Second Innings.	
1 Makepeace b Rhodes ...	... 17	c Robinson b Kilner ...	9
5 A. W Pewtress b Macaulay ...	... 20	b Macaulay ...	5
3 Tyldesley, E. lbw Macaulay ..	... 29	c Waddington b Kilner ...	2
4 Watson c Waddington b Rhodes	... 13	lbw Kilner ...	... 21
2 Hallows lbw Macaulay ...	... 5	lbw Rhodes ...	0
6 J. Sharp b Kilner	.. 12	c & b Kilner ...	... 14
7 Iddon b Macaulay ...	... 6	b Rhodes ...	4
8 A. Rhodes c Oldroyd b Macaulay	... 1	b Macaulay ...	6
9 Tyldesley, R. c Holmes b Kilner	... 3	b Macaulay ...	0
10 Parkin lbw Macaulay ...	... 0	not out ...	2
11 Duckworth not out ...	... 0	c Robinson b Macaulay ...	0
	Extras 7	Extras	11

Total runs at fall of each wicket   Total 113   Total 74
7 33 65 65 82 102 107 111 113 113 | 7 16 32 41 41 53 69 69 72 74

Bowler	Overs	Maidens	Runs	W'k'ts	Overs	Maidens	Runs	W'k'ts
Robinson ...	11	7	10	0	2	1	3	0
Macaulay ..	33	14	40	6	16·2	7	19	4
Kilner, R. ...	26·2	12	28	2	23	16	13	4
Rhodes ...	20	7	28	2	15	5	28	2

YORKSHIRE.

First Innings.			Second Innings.	
1 Holmes b Parkin	 10	lbw Tyldesley R.	... 0
2 Sutcliffe c Tyldesley R. b Parkin	.. 0	lbw Parkin ...	... 3
3 Oldroyd b Tyldesley R. ...	... 37	b Parkin ...	... 3
4 Leyland run out ...	... 21	c & b Tyldesley R.	... 0
5 Rhodes lbw Parkin ...	... 18	c Makepeace b Tyldesley R.	7
6 Kilner, R. b Parkin ...	... 35	not out ...	... 13
7 Robinson c & b Parkin ...	... 1	run out ...	... 2
8 Turner lbw Tyldesley R. ...	... 6	b Tyldesley R. ...	1
9 Macaulay c & b Tyldesley R. ..	... 0	b Parkin ...	... 4
10 Waddington b Tyldesley R. ..	... 0	b Tyldesley R. ...	0
11 Dolphin not out ...	... 0	st Duckworth b Tyldesley R.	0
	Extras 6	Extras	

Total runs at fall of each wicket   Total 130   Total 33
3 10 68 87 97 115 120 120 126 130 | 3 3 3 13 13 16 23 32 33 33

Bowler	Overs	Maidens	Runs	W'k'ts	Overs	Maidens	Runs	W'k'ts
Parkin ...	27·2	9	46	5	12	7	15	3
Tyldesley, R.	27	9	69	4	11·5	6	18	6
Watson	7	2	9	0				

Umpires : Messrs. Chester & Warren   Scorers   Messrs Ringrose & Moore.   Commence Sat. 12, Mon. & Tues. 11-30.   Lunch 1-45 to 2-30.   Stumps drawn 6-30.

Printed on the Ground by Arthur Wigley The Waverley Press. Woodhouse Street, Leeds

The Yorkshire-Lancashire score card of the match at Headingley, Leeds, in 1924, when Yorkshire wanting only 58 runs to win were dismissed by Dick Tyldesley and Cecil Parkin for a mere 33, losing the match by 24 runs.

47

Roy Kilner, a Yorkshire hero of pre and post-war days. One of the most popular ever of cricketers, this left-hand batsman and slow left-arm bowler, died at the height of his career in the spring of 1928, soon after returning from a coaching engagement in India.

This picture shows Roy Kilner's grave in Wombwell Cemetery, where he was buried in April 1928. It is estimated that over 150,000 people lined the streets of Wombwell to watch the funeral procession and pay their last tributes to this great Yorkshire and England cricketer.

The great Wilfred Rhodes in the later days of his cricketing career.

Do you recognise this youngster? Arthur Mitchell was for many years part of the backbone of the Yorkshire batting and the successor to Edgar Oldroyd as the "number three." Also a brilliant close-in fielder, Mitchell later became Yorkshire's senior coach.

This is a picture of another in the line of great Yorkshire wicket-keepers, Arthur Wood, taken as a choir boy. Wood kept wicket for Yorkshire in 222 successive county championship matches between 1928 and 1935.

Famous Yorkshire coach, George Hirst, seen with some of the colts in the late 1920s during a coaching session at Headingley. The group includes:— back row (left to right), Dennis, Bowes, Jacques, and Davidson; front row (left to right), Barber, Bedford and Fisher. All these colts eventually played for the county.

Brian Sellers and George Macaulay lead out the Yorkshire team in a county match at Headingley in 1935.

The Yorkshire Committee grouped at Headingley just before the start of the 1932 season.

Back Row: Mr. Heyhirst (Trainer) L. Hutton H. Verity W. E. Bowes T. F. Smailes C. Turner A. Wood Mr. Rincrose (Scorer)

Front Row: W. Barber   H. Sutcliffe   A. B. Sellers (Capt.)   M. Leyland   A. Mitchell

Another Yorkshire team picture, the side of 1936, which finished third in the county championship table.

A fine picture of Yorkshire's great left arm bowler between the wars, Hedley Verity. He died of wounds in July, 1943.

Yorkshire cricketers, Sellers, Leyland and Smailes, already "joined up,"
but still in mufti, soon after the outbreak of World War 2.

The Post-War Years

YORKSHIRE were back in the field again in 1946, even if with a side of changed personnel. Sellers was still at the helm and by the end of the season the county side were at the top of the championship table. N. W. D. Yardley, who had first played for Yorkshire in 1936 and had scored three centuries pre-war, became an established batsman—and sometimes, bowler—for the county side and later led England in Test Matches. He captained Yorkshire for eight seasons, but only once—in 1949—were the side top of the table, and then equal with Middlesex. Yet, five times, Yorkshire finished in second place, and the early '50s saw the development of those great Yorkshire Cricketing characters, Close and Trueman.

When Yardley relinquished the captaincy after the 1955 season, Yorkshire had three different captains in the space of five years, with the last, J. V. Wilson, being Yorkshire's first professional captain since the 1880s. Yorkshire had to wait 10 years, from 1949 to 1959, before winning the championship again. Their leader was J. R. Burnet, brought in to the side in the previous year at the age of 39. Yet throughout this period, new youngsters were gaining experience in the team, notably Wardle, (successor to Verity), D. V. Brennan, as wicket-keeper, Appleyard and Illingworth. All were to play for England.

In the '60s, some of Yorkshire's riches fell away. players retired, and others found fame elsewhere. Close became Yorkshire's captain in 1963 and four times led the side to the top of the championship table, before he disappeared from the scene in 1971. Yorkshire lost Trueman, who retired in 1968, as well as Illingworth, who left to play for—and captain—Leicestershire and England. In the following year, Binks, who had followed Brennan as Yorkshire's wicket-keeper for 15 years, also retired from the first class game. The steam seemed to have gone out of Yorkshire cricket, with the side finishing as low as 12th in 1969.

When Close left, it was to Boycott to whom Yorkshire turned as leader, but 1971, 1972 and 1973 still saw the county side low down the table. It was obvious that team building was a slow process, despite some success in the various one-day competitions that had now become a part of the English cricket scene. For a time Sharpe, Hampshire, Padgett and Don Wilson, among others, had kept Yorkshire on the top, but once the slide had commenced it was to young players like Lumb, Bairstow and Old that the county side needed to turn.

An historic picture. Here are Herbert Sutcliffe and his son, Billy, opening
the innings together for Pudsey Britannia against East Leeds in 1944.

Norman Yardley (left), captain of England, and Alan Melville, captain of South Africa, returning from making the toss in a Test Match in 1947.

An ideal stance for any young cricketer to copy. Sir Leonard Hutton at the wicket at the North Marine enclosure at Scarborough.

Back Row L. to R.: B. Heyhirst (Masseur), H. Halliday, G. A. Smithson, J. V. Wilson, R. Aspinall, E. Lester, H. L. Walker (Scorer)

Front Row L. to R.: W. Watson, A. Coxon, D. V. Brennan, N. W. D. Yardley (Capt.), L. Hutton, E. P. Robinson, J. H. Wardle

The Yorkshire Team of 1949. In this year, Yorkshire finished top of the county championship table, sharing the honours with Middlesex.

Wilfred Rhodes bowls at the opening of the new cricket ground at Silcoates School, Wakefield, in 1949. It is believed this is the last ball ever delivered by the great Yorkshire left arm bowler.

T. L. Taylor, President of the Yorkshire County Cricket Club, chats to
Vic Wilson (left) and Bob Appleyard at the pre-season nets in 1955.

J. H. Wardle, Yorkshire's popular left arm slow bowler and hard-hitting batsman. Played from 1946 to 1958.

A happy group of Yorkshire cricketers and friends taken on a social occasion in 1959.

Freddie Trueman, the Yorkshire and England fast bowler, looks up at his portrait in oils, painted by Ruskin Spear, at the Royal Academy's summer exhibition in 1965.

The gates erected at Headingley in 1965 to the great Yorkshire and England batsman, Herbert Sutcliffe.

Yorkshire, winners of the Gillette Cup for the first time in 1965, when they beat Surrey. The Captain, Brian Close, joyfully holds the trophy aloft.

Captains all! Taken at the pre-season lunch at Headingley, Leeds, in 1966. From left to right: J. R. Burnet, N. W. D. Yardley, Sir William Worsley, A. B. Sellers, D. B. Close, and W. H. H. Sutcliffe.

Sir William Worsley Bt. of Hovingham, York,
President of the Yorkshire County Cricket Club,
taken in 1967.

The scene of many happy end-of-season games. A fine panoramic view of
the North Marine enclosure at Scarborough.

74   A general view of the Headingley Cricket Ground, Leeds, taken from the
Kirkstall Lane end, as it was in 1956.

Another view of the ground showing the new players' pavilion.

Bramall Lane Cricket Ground at Sheffield, taken in 1971.

Back Row left to right: G. Cope, G. Boycott, N. Smith, C. Old, R. Hutton, J. Hampshire, B. Leadbeater, J. Woodford

Front Row left to right: D. Wilson, P. Sharpe, B. Close, D. Padgett, T. Nicholson

The Yorkshire team of 1970—Close's last season as captain.

Back Row L. to R.: J. Woodford, M. K. Bore, B. Leadbeater, R. G. Lumb, R. Hutton, C. Old, J. H. Hampshire, G. A. Cope, A. J. Dalton
Front Row L. to R.: N. Smith, A. G. Nicholson, D. Wilson, G. Boycott, D. Padgett, P. Sharpe, D. Bairstow

The Yorkshire team of 1971.

Former Yorkshire cricketers in a get-together at Leeds in 1967. Left to right: Bill Bowes, Norman Yardley, Sandy Jacques, Frank Smailes, Sir William Worsley and Arthur Wood.

Geoffrey Boycott. A fine close-up of the present Yorkshire captain.